FUN FACT FILE: EARTH SCIENCE

20 FUN FACTS ABOUT WEATHER

By Caitie McAneney

Gareth Stevens PUBLISHING

Please visit our website, www.garethstevens.com. For a free color catalog of all our high-quality books, call toll free 1-800-542-2595 or fax 1-877-542-2596.

Cataloging-in-Publication Data

Names: McAneney, Caitie.
Title: 20 fun facts about weather / Caitie McAneney.
Description: New York : Gareth Stevens Publishing, 2018. | Series: Fun fact file: earth science | Includes index.
Identifiers: ISBN 9781538211939 (pbk.) | ISBN 9781538211953 (library bound) | ISBN 9781538211946 (6 pack)
Subjects: LCSH: Weather--Juvenile literature.
Classification: LCC QC981.3 M286 2018 | DDC 551.5--dc23

First Edition

Published in 2018 by
Gareth Stevens Publishing
111 East 14th Street, Suite 349
New York, NY 10003

Designer: Sam DeMartin
Editor: Joan Stoltman

Photo credits: Cover, p. 1 Dudarev Mikhail/Shutterstock.com; p. 5 solarseven/Shutterstock.com; p. 6 Denis Burdin/Shutterstock.com; p. 7 The Asahi Shimbum Premium/The Asahi Shimbum/Getty Images; p. 8 Topical Press Agency/Hulton Archive/Getty Images; p. 9 Hindustan Times/Hindustan Times/Getty Images; p. 10 Tad Denson/Shutterstock.com; p. 11 (right) Brian Nolan/Shutterstock.com; p. 11 (left) Chuck Wagner/Shutterstock.com; p. 11 (timeline) world of vector/Shutterstock.com; p. 12 Mario Tama/Getty Images News/Getty Images; p. 13 Buyenlarge/Archive Photos/Getty Images; p. 14 Scott Olsen/Getty Images News/Getty Images; p. 15 Portland Press Herald/Portland Press Herald/Getty Images; p. 16 John G. White/Denver Post/Getty Images; p. 17 welcomia/Shutterstock.com; p. 18 Brendon Thorne/Getty Images News/Getty Images; p. 19 Mimadeo/Shutterstock.com; p. 20 Ahmad A. Atwah/Shutterstock.com; p. 21 Mvuijlst/Shutterstock.com; pp. 22, 23 Minerva Studio/Shutterstock.com; p. 24 Leo Pinheiro/Shutterstock.com; p. 25 Harry Beugelink/Shutterstock.com; p. 26 NASA Images/Shutterstock.com; p. 27 (glacier) Bernhard Staehli/Shutterstock.com; p. 27 (cracked ground) 24Novembers/Shutterstock.com; p. 27 (water levels) Imfoto/Shutterstock.com; p. 29 Alex Kosev/Shutterstock.com.

Printed in the United States of America

CPSIA compliance information: Batch #CW18GS: For further information contact Gareth Stevens, New York, New York at 1-800-542-2595.

Contents

Weird Weather 4
All About Rain 6
Fearsome Floods 8
Horrible Hurricanes 10
Scary Snowstorms 14
Wicked Winds 18
Deadly Dust Storms 20
Terrible Tornadoes 22
Bizarre Bolts 24
Climate Change 26
A Force of Nature 28
Glossary 30
For More Information 31
Index 32

Words in the glossary appear in **bold** type the first time they are used in the text.

Weird Weather

Earth is home to some really weird weather! There are sunny days, and there are days with lots of snow, rain, and wind. Sometimes it's very hot, and sometimes it's so cold you can't go outside! Long-term patterns of weather are called climates. Climates are different depending where on Earth you are.

Sometimes weather is even dangerous. People can't control these forces of nature. What we can do is listen to storm warnings and stay safe during storms.

Storms can cause major damage, or harm, to roads, buildings, and homes.

There are four kinds of deserts, and three of them have cold or cool climates.

FACT 1

The world's largest desert is the continent of Antarctica.

We usually picture hot, sandy places when we think of deserts. But there are also cold deserts! Antarctica gets less than 10 inches (25 cm) of yearly precipitation, or water falling from the sky. That's dry enough to be called a desert!

FACT 2

The northeastern Indian village of Mawsynram may be the rainiest place on Earth.

Many countries have a rainy season each year! During the rainy season, Mawsynram gets between 450 inches and 700 inches (1,140 and 1,780 cm).

People who live in Mawsynram wear baskets shaped like turtle shells to keep dry during the rainy season.

Fearsome Floods

FACT 3

In 1931, a terrible flood in China covered an area bigger than the country of England!

When huge amounts of melting snow and pouring rain overfilled China's great rivers, it became one of the deadliest **natural disasters** ever. Over 50 million people lost their homes, and as many as 3.7 million may have died.

The floodwaters in China also spread illnesses and ruined food supplies and crops.

FACT 4

During India's 2016 monsoon season, floodwaters reached higher than some tall buildings!

A monsoon is a strong, seasonal storm that causes months of heavy rain. India is famous for its monsoon season, which often includes flooding. When floodwaters rose to more than 164 feet (50 m) in some places, they broke flooding records!

Sometimes monsoon flooding in India is so bad that hundreds of thousands of people are forced to move.

Horrible Hurricanes

The damage from Hurricane Katrina cost over $ 108 billion. Many people lost everything, including homes, cars, and clothes.

FACT 5

Hurricanes are huge, spinning storms that can have winds nearly 160 miles (260 km) per hour.

In 2005, Hurricane Katrina hit Florida, Mississippi, Alabama, Georgia, and Louisiana. The hardest-hit area was New Orleans, where **levees** broke and flooded the city.

This timeline shows the events of Hurricane Katrina in 2005.

Hurricane Katrina Timeline

August 24
Tropical Storm Katrina appears off Florida.

August 25
With 75 mile-an-hour (120 kph) winds, the tropical storm is now a hurricane.

August 26
100 mile-an-hour (160 kph) winds.

August 27
115 mile-an-hour (185 kph) winds. Warnings in Mississippi and Louisiana.

August 28
160 mile-an-hour (260 kph) winds. The sea could rise 28 feet (8.5 m), so people are told to leave the area. Many people are unable to leave.

August 29
Hurricane Katrina hits New Orleans.

August 30
As levees break, New Orleans floods.

September 1
Troops are sent to save people.

Hurricane Sandy ruined this theme park on the shores of New Jersey.

FACT 6

Because Hurricane Sandy was so huge, it was also called Superstorm Sandy and Frankenstorm!

In October 2012, Hurricane Sandy hit the Caribbean, causing great damage in countries like Haiti. Then, it traveled up the US East Coast, reaching New York City and New Jersey. A wave in New York Harbor was measured at 32.5 feet (9.9 m)!

FACT 7

In 1900, the storm surge of a hurricane raised the sea level 15 feet (4.6 m)!

When the Galveston Hurricane hit the Texas coast on September 8, 1900, there was little warning. In fact, the warning system used in Galveston at that time was a man in a horse-drawn cart!

Winds likely reached more than 120 miles (193 km) per hour at times during the Galveston Hurricane.

FACT 8

The word "blizzard" was first used for a snowstorm in an Iowa newspaper in the 1870s.

Many places in the Northern **Hemisphere** have snowstorms in the winter. A blizzard is a storm with blowing snow and low **visibility**. When winds of more than 35 miles (56 km) an hour blow the snow around, no one can see!

There doesn't need to be a lot of snow for a blizzard to happen! If drivers can't see when on the road because of blowing snow, it might be a blizzard.

The blizzard even hit states like Alabama and Tennessee that hardly ever see snow.

FACT 9

A superstorm in 1993 became known as the "Storm of the Century."

A blizzard in 1993 was one of the largest winter storms ever! A **cyclone** brought tons of snow from the Southeast to the Northeast United States. More than 10 million people lost power!

FACT 10

Some snowdrifts from the Super Bowl Blizzard of 1975 reached over 20 feet (6 m) tall!

The blizzard got its name because it took place just days before the biggest football game of the year. The same storm system that covered the Midwest in snow created **tornadoes** that ran across the Southeast.

The blizzard didn't stop the Super Bowl from being played in New Orleans, Louisiana, but it may have stopped some fans from getting to the game!

FACT 11

Silver Lake, Colorado, holds the US record for the most snowfall in 24 hours.

In 1921, a huge snowstorm hit Silver Lake with more than 6 feet (1.8 m) of snow in one day. That's taller than most people!

FACT 12

The fastest wind gust ever recorded on Earth's surface was more than 250 miles (400 km) per hour.

A strong, short burst of wind is called a gust. During **Typhoon** Olivia in 1996, Barrow Island, Australia, was hit by a gust traveling 253 miles (407 km) per hour!

Sydney, Australia in 2015

Strong winds can cause a lot of damage by throwing heavy objects—and even people!—around.

Wind is made into energy using machines called wind turbines.

FACT 13

Wind can be used as power.

People have used wind to power sailboats for more than 5,000 years. Today, we can use wind to make electricity! Wind is known as a renewable resource, which means it'll always be around for us to use.

Deadly Dust Storms

FACT 14

Strong winds that can cause walls of sand in the air are called "haboobs" in Arabic.

When high winds happen in a desert, it's called a sandstorm. Sandstorms can sweep over towns and cities. People can have trouble seeing and breathing outside during a sandstorm.

Haboobs mostly happen in the southern Sahara Desert.

FACT 15

In the 1930s, dust storms blew across the middle of the United States for 8 years!

The middle of the United States badly needed rain. Dust storms covered a large area across several states that become known as the Dust Bowl. Dirt filled the air, sometimes even blocking the sun!

Many farmers had to just leave their land and homes behind during the Dust Bowl.

Terrible Tornadoes

States that are part of Tornado Alley include Oklahoma, Texas, Kansas, and Nebraska.

FACT 16

The United States has around 1,000 tornadoes a year—more than any other country in the world!

The wind inside a tornado can reach 300 miles (483 km) per hour. Tornadoes often happen as part of huge thunderstorms called supercells. Part of the United States is called Tornado Alley because there are so many tornadoes!

FACT 17

Waterspouts can rain frogs and fish from the sky!

Waterspouts are made when air spins quickly over open water. They can pick up animals while they're over water. Then the water actually drops back down from clouds into the air.

One kind of waterspout, called a fair-weather waterspout, doesn't move. Tornadic waterspouts, though, are actually strong, moving tornadoes over water.

Bizarre Bolts

FACT 18

A flash of lightning can make the air around it five times hotter than the sun's surface.

Lightning bolts are made of dangerous amounts of quickly moving electricity that can heat or burn anything in its way. Lightning can sometimes strike over 10 miles (16 km) from the storm cloud where it started.

The average American has about a 1 in 5,000 chance of being struck by lightning during their lifetime.

FACT 19

When lightning hits a tree, the tree may explode!

When lightning hits a tree, the heat quickly turns the water inside the tree to vapor. This creates steam, which can blow the tree apart!

Lightning can happen within clouds, or it can strike from a cloud to the ground.

FACT 20

You can affect Earth's climates!

Climate change is a change in weather patterns over time, caused partly by human activities like burning oil and coal. It makes for hotter and colder temperatures than ever, which feeds storms and leads to harmful weather.

a typhoon from space

What you do makes a difference. Think before you act!

What Does Climate Change Do?

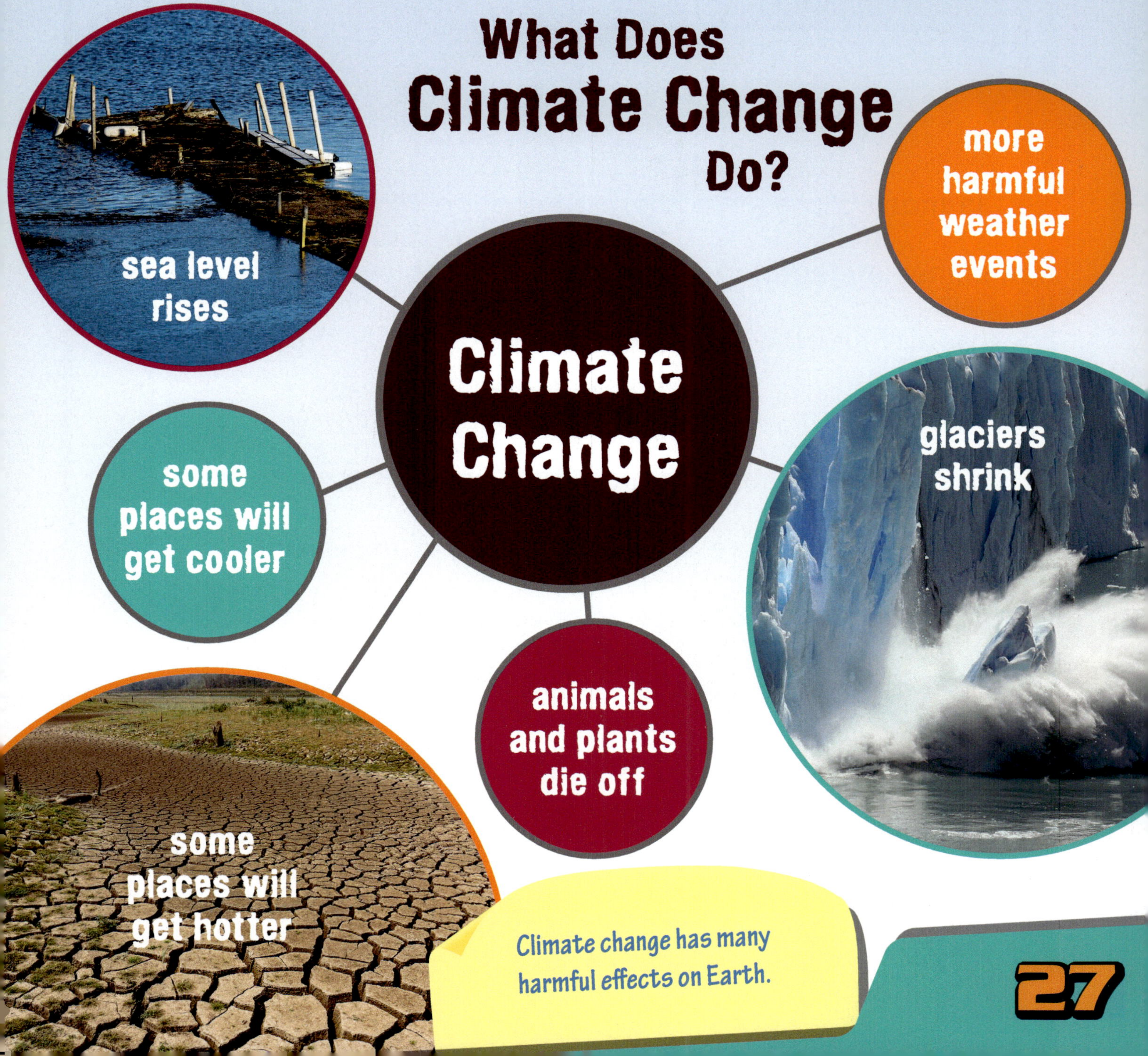

Climate change has many harmful effects on Earth.

A Force of Nature

In many places, weather can change very quickly! Sometimes meteorologists, or scientists who study weather, can **predict** future weather. Other times, it takes them by surprise, too!

Because of climate change, bad weather may happen more often in the future. Be prepared! Pack important supplies, such as food, water, clothing, and a radio. Head to a safe place if you're told to do so. While in safety, pay attention to TV or radio news to know when the weather has passed!

To prepare for a storm, have cans of food and a can opener, flashlights, batteries, tools, water, and a first aid kit packed or nearby.

Glossary

continent: one of Earth's seven great landmasses

cyclone: a large, powerful, damaging storm with strong, spinning winds

levee: a long wall of soil built along a river to prevent flooding

natural disaster: a sudden and terrible event in nature that causes damage and death

hemisphere: one half of the Earth

predict: to guess what will happen in the future based on facts or knowledge

tornado: a storm with powerful winds that spin around a central point and cause damage

typhoon: a type of cyclone that happens near the equator

visibility: how far you are able to see because of weather or darkness

For More Information

Books

Furgang, Kathy. *Everything Weather*. Washington, DC: National Geographic, 2012.

Manolis, Kay. *Blizzards*. Minnetonka, MN: Bellwether Media, 2016.

Schuh, Mari C. *Tsunamis*. Mankato, MN: Capstone Press, 2016.

Websites

Earth Science for Kids: Weather—Tornadoes
ducksters.com/science/earth_science/tornadoes.php
Discover one of the most powerful kinds of weather—tornadoes!

National Geographic: Hurricane
kids.nationalgeographic.com/explore/science/hurricane
Learn all about hurricanes!

Weather for Kids
weatherforkids.org
Explore different kinds of fascinating weather events!

Index

Antarctica 6
blizzard 14, 15, 16
climate change 26, 27, 28
climates 4, 26
cyclone 15
desert 6, 20
Dust Bowl 21
dust storms 21
flood 8, 9, 11
Galveston Hurricane 13
haboobs 20
Hurricane Katrina 10, 11
hurricanes 10, 11, 13
Hurricane Sandy 12
lightning 24, 25
Mawsynram 7
monsoon 9
precipitation 6
rain 4, 7, 8, 9, 21, 23
sandstorms 20
snow 4, 8, 14, 15, 16, 17
Super Bowl Blizzard 16
Tornado Alley 22
tornadoes 16, 22, 23
Typhoon Olivia 18
waterspouts 23
wind 4, 11, 13, 14, 18, 19, 20, 22